WILLIAM HENRY HARRISON AND OTHER POEMS

For Loren

WILLIAM HENRY HARRISON
AND
OTHER POEMS

DAVID R. SLAVITT

with kind regard —

[signature]

4/11/07

LOUISIANA STATE UNIVERSITY PRESS
BATON ROUGE

Published by Louisiana State University Press
Copyright © 2006 by David R. Slavitt
Manufactured in the United States of America
First printing

DESIGNER: Barbara Neely Bourgoyne
TYPEFACE: Adobe Caslon Pro
PRINTER AND BINDER: Edwards Brothers, Inc.

LIBRARY OF CONGRESS CATALOGING-IN-PUBLICATION DATA

Slavitt, David R., 1935–
  William Henry Harrison and other poems / David R. Slavitt.
    p. cm.
  ISBN 0-8071-3120-2 (alk. paper) — ISBN 0-8071-3121-0 (pbk. : alk. paper)
  1. Harrison, William Henry, 1773–1841—Poetry. I. Title.
PS3569.L3W55 2006
811'.54—dc22

                                              2005014398

Some of these poems have appeared in *Hudson Review, New Criterion, Texas Review,*
  Poetry, Denver Quarterly, Main Street Rag, and the *New York Times.*

The paper in this book meets the guidelines for permanence and durability
of the Committee on Production Guidelines for Book Longevity
of the Council on Library Resources.
∞

For Janet

Contents

WILLIAM HENRY HARRISON AND OTHER POEMS

William Henry Harrison

William Henry Harrison.

With the three names like that, it sounds as though his mother is calling him and she's really angry. William Henry Harrison, you come here right this minute. And wash your hands and face. With soap!

Is that unfair? Perhaps, but what other president insisted on all three names? Chester Alan Arthur, maybe. But he used the initial: Chester A. Arthur. And that always sounds wrong. "Chester, *an* Arthur" is what one wants to say.

You've never wanted to say that? I am prepared to believe you, although it could mean that I think less of you. (Less of you than I did before, not less of you than of Chester an Arthur, who does crop up every now and then.) Harrison crops up, too, but less frequently.

For John Quincy Adams, we use all three names, but that is only to distinguish him from his father. And for the same reason, we use George W. Bush's middle initial, to distinguish him from his father, with whom of course he shares not only the initial but the middle name. (What really distinguishes Dubya is that he doesn't have the *H* for Herbert.)

(There's also William Howard Taft, but he had such gravitas. Or call it, more bluntly, fatness. Still, he qualifies as a true trinomial.)

Harrison, William Henry is what he would be in a card catalogue. But somewhere else in the catalogue, there could well be a William, Henry Harrison. (Or, more likely, Williams, Henry Harrison?) And in what boasts of itself as the real world, there are likely to have been any number of people named Harrison William Henry.

They're all common enough, both as first and last names, which is odd. A
tough row to hoe, carrying the names of a president that way. But at least
Harrison, William Henry was a relatively obscure president.

His relative—grandson actually—Benjamin Harrison was relatively obscure, too.

Harrison Benjamin is also a perfectly plausible name.

We can imagine Harrison Ford and Richard Benjamin in *Tippecanoe!*
What we can't imagine is their making such a movie, although it could
be a very good movie. (Which is, in part, what militates against it.) But
a movie about Indian fighting (or militation?) would be politically
incorrect. Hand-to-hand combat on the bank of the Wabash with
the valiant general killing the screaming savages . . .?

How would the poor screen writers tap-dance their way around that? We
luxuriate in a guilt we don't really feel, and the Indians, these days, have to
be the good guys. *Tap-Dancing with Wolves*. With Buck Henry. And Rex
Harrison. And out there, performing a synchronized swimming routine
in the river, while the bullets whine and the arrows fly, is that . . .? Yes, it's
Esther Williams!

2

We have had other joke presidents. Calvin Coolidge was a joke, except that, as
Hoover discovered when the Depression hit, it was Coolidge who had the
last laugh.

Millard Fillmore was a joke. "In my view," Fillmore said, "secession on the part
of the southern states would be illegal; but, should the southern states
secede, I do not understand that there is anything the northern states can
legally do about it."

It is not impossible, however, that Fillmore was making a joke, and that if we'd known how to laugh at it, the butchery of the Civil War might have been avoided. And we'd have had a Fillmore penny.

Clinton wasn't so much a joke as an embarrassment.

But Harrison was a joke. The joke is that he gave the longest inaugural address in our history. On a cold day in Washington, he spoke for an hour and three-quarters and caught cold, which turned into pneumonia, which killed him, so that his was the shortest administration in our history.

It's what you know about him. It's probably all you know about him. And it's not true, although it makes a good story. But leaving a space that way, Harrison invites us to fill it any way we like. His is a phantom administration, eliciting from each of us whatever is within us. His is, therefore, the most scrupulously democratic presidency.

3

All promise and no fulfillment. Or, all promise and no betrayal. Knowing what was to follow upon that inauguration, we cannot help but read his words differently and more ominously: "The outline of principles to govern and measures to be adopted by an Administration not yet begun will soon be exchanged for immutable history, and I shall stand either exonerated by my countrymen or classed with the mass of those who promised that they might deceive and flattered with the intention to betray."

Too refined for the office? Or for the world? He disdained the sordid occupation of actually running a country. He was perhaps dismayed by having been the first president whose campaign used a slogan. Can you imagine Washington with a slogan? Or Augustus Caesar? Or Pericles?

His was the first modern campaign, not only with a slogan but with image
mongering. Harrison was presented as the log-cabin type, a simple
fellow who liked to sit and swill cider. He was already venturing into
fiction because he was an aristocrat whose father had signed the
Declaration of Independence and had been governor of Virginia.

It is tempting to suggest that mortification was what he died of. The
pneumonia was merely the means, what the doctors could understand,
or could declare without actually insulting the electorate.

A month in office, and then he steps out of time to soar into an ether in which
he has a ghostly existence with a face that appears on postage stamps and
that reversible name that gets listed in almanacs. It isn't exactly fame. Or it's
a modest, tasteful fame, as if he'd won the Pulitzer Prize for poetry.

It's a negative fame. One could argue that no administration has been as
scandal-free as that of William Henry Harrison.

The honeymoon, then the illness, then the eulogies. An unblemished record.
One thinks of those infants in Brazil who die in their first days or weeks
and whose mothers think of them as angels too fastidious to survive in this
imperfect world.

Having no evidence to the contrary, we can assume that Harrison was sincere
in his distaste for power. He said of it, in that Inaugural Address: "When
this corrupting passion once takes possession of the human mind, like the
love of gold it becomes insatiable. It is the never-dying worm in his bosom,
grows with his growth and strengthens with the declining years of its vic-
tim. If this is true, it is the part of wisdom for a republic to limit the service
of that officer at least to whom she has intrusted the management of her
foreign relations, the execution of her laws, and the command of her armies
and navies to a period so short as to prevent his forgetting that he is the

accountable agent, not the principal; the servant, not the master. Until an amendment of the Constitution can be effected public opinion may secure the desired object. I give my aid to it by renewing the pledge heretofore given that under no circumstances will I consent to serve a second term."

As it turned out, he was spared even having to serve much of a first term.

4

His featurelessness is his hallmark. Like the heads on Easter Island, he stares out with blank eyes, defying time and braving the weather that cannot erode his features any further. He is unintimidated, unimpressed.

There are portraits, statues, and bas reliefs, but he recedes into them, a conventionally handsome, well-groomed, elderly man who might have been plucked off the wall of the administration building of some college—a dean of students or chairman of the classics department. He has one of those generic faces that is difficult to recall from moment to moment. Blink, and he is gone.

He prefers it that way.

What he cannot altogether escape is his grandson's fame. Benjamin Harrison was president, too, defeating President Grover Cleveland in 1888 in what was until then the most corrupt campaign in the nation's history. It was less a victory for Harrison than it was a repudiation of Cleveland.

It was a close election. Cleveland won 90,000 more popular votes. But not in the right places. Harrison, who was for high tariffs, won the manufacturing states, and a few important swing states.

Benjamin Harrison was a one-term president, but not because he had
his grandfather's principles. He ran again in 1892, but this time the
electorate, repudiating him, re-elected Grover Cleveland.

So Benjamin Harrison was a joke president, too, but as in most jokes, shorter
is better.

5

Even now, when the Native Americans are always the good guys and white
men are the villains, William Henry Harrison's conduct at Tippecanoe
seems unexceptionable.

Harrison did not attack the Indians; they attacked him.

Tecumseh claimed that the sale of Indiana land to white men by the
Miamies was not legal and valid unless endorsed by a confederacy of all
the Indians of the confederacy—the Shawnee, Canadian Iroquois, Wyan-
dot, Mingo, Ottawa, Chickamauga, Miami, Kickapoo, Delaware, Ojibwa,
Potawatomi, Fox, Sauk, and Mascouten.

Harrison answered that "when the white people arrived on this continent,
they found the Miamies in the occupation of all the country in the
Wabash, and at that time the Shawanees were residents of Georgia, from
which they were driven by the Creeks. The lands have been
purchased from the Miamies, who were the true and original owners
of it. It is ridiculous to assert that all the Indians are one nation, for
if such had been the intention of the Great Spirit, he would not have put
six different tongues into their heads, but would have taught
them all to speak one language."

Abandoning all languages, Tecumseh leapt up and threatened Harrison with
a war club. Harrison said in a calm but firm voice that Tecumseh was

"a bad man," that he would have no further talk with him, and that he should now depart from the settlements immediately. Tecumseh left, but the Indians were not satisfied.

Under the leadership of Tecumseh and Elskwatawa, his brother, often called "the Prophet," the Indians gathered to resist the white man's incursions. They robbed and burned houses, stole horses, and killed settlers. Governor Harrison petitioned President Madison and finally received permission to march against the Prophet's town with an armed force, but to avoid hostilities "of any kind or any degree, not indispensably required."

At Tippecanoe where Harrison had encamped, the Prophet ordered an attack before dawn. He did not join in himself but on a nearby hill chanted his incantations, having assured his followers that the Great Spirit would turn the Americans' bullets into drops of water.

It wasn't just the charm he was counting on, though. There was also surprise. And the battle was a near thing and messy, as hand-to-hand combat always is. Sixty-two killed and a hundred and twenty-six wounded. Almost a fifth of Harrison's force were casualties. A bullet passed through the rim of Harrison's hat.

But the Indians were driven off. They decamped and dispersed. And Harrison was a hero.

6

He said that he would be a one-term president. He also said that he would not veto any legislation unless he thought it was unconstitutional. And that he would propose none to the congress. This was not the business of the executive branch.

In a radical way, he saw himself not as a governor but as the president, whose job, therefore, was not to govern, which is active and intrusive, but more delicately and modestly merely to preside. He thought of himself as the nation's chief magistrate.

In 1829, President John Quincy Adams had sent him as a special envoy to Colombia. There, he saw what Simón Bolívar had done, assuming despotic powers over what he took to be an ungovernable rabble.

Harrison wrote a long letter to Bolívar warning him of the risk both to Bolivia and to himself that he would incur by assuming totalitarian powers. Addressing Bolívar as one general to another, he said, "Depend upon it, sir, that the moment which shall announce the continuance of arbitrary powers in your hands, will be the commencement of commotions which will require all your talents and energies to suppress. You may succeed. The disciplined army, at your disposal, may be too powerful for an unarmed, undisciplined, and scattered population; but one unsuccessful effort will not content them, and your feelings will be eternally racked by being obliged to make war upon those who have been accustomed to call you their father, and to invoke blessings on your head, and for no cause but their adherence to principles which you yourself had taught them to regard more than their lives."

Rousing stuff. But it accomplished less than nothing, for Bolívar paid no attention to the letter from the idealistic Yankee. And Bolivians, who remember William Henry Harrison better than we do, hate him for having insulted their hero.

That he was absolutely accurate only makes his remarks more insulting. He asked Bolívar, "will the pomp and glitter of a court, and the flattery of venal courtiers, reward you for the troubles and anxieties attendant upon the exercise of sovereignty, everywhere . . .? Or power supported by the bayonet, for that willing homage which you were wont to receive from your fellow-citizens? The groans of a dissatisfied and oppressed people will penetrate the inmost recesses of your palace, and you will be tortured by the reflection that you no longer possess that place in their affections, which was once your pride and your boast, and which would have been your solace under every reverse of fortune. Unsupported by the people, your authority can be maintained, only, by the terrors of the sword and the scaffold. And have these ever been successful under similar circumstances? Blood may smother, for a period, but can never extinguish, the fire of liberty, which you have contributed so much to kindle, in the bosom of every Colombian."

7

At his inauguration, on March 4, Harrison wore neither overcoat nor gloves and was bareheaded. It was a chilly day and there was a northeast wind, but it is unlikely that it killed him.

Can you "take a chill?" Do you "catch cold" from being cold? Has the germ theory not yet caught on?

His health seems not to have been impaired until sometime after the 26th. He had walked out through slush a day or two before that. And he had been caught in a sudden shower on his way to Lafayette Square to offer a diplomatic post to a Colonel John Tayloe.

It was not until March 27th that he sent for a physician. The president was "extensively cupped," and the doctors announced that he had "bilious pleurisy."

It is altogether appropriate for a nearly fictional president to expire of a fictional disease.

After a week in bed, he felt better and requested that the 103rd Psalm be read in thanksgiving for his recovery.

But there was a relapse. On April 3, the four attending physicians pronounced him as "beyond recovery."

The patient sank into a stupor. In his delirium, he was heard by Colonel George Groghan, who was sitting at the president's bedside, to say, "It is wrong. I won't consent. 'Tis unjust." And then, perhaps related and perhaps not, "These applications, will they never cease?"

A Dr. N. W. Worthington, however, reported that his last words were, "Sir, I wish you to understand the true principles of the government. I wish them carried out. I ask nothing more."

This is an obvious invention. The doctor could see that the door was already open. It remains open.

8

His spirit was freed, as our spirits are, too, so that we can imagine, if we please, the oratorio with a thousand voices in close harmony, singing his praises, addressing the box that is always empty because, even if he were alive, he would have shunned such a display.

You say you have never heard of such a performance? Not, perhaps, in the real world, but there ought to be. On February 9, which is his birthday, we should have odes and threnes, dithyrambs and dirges. And sambas, because it happens also to be Carmen Miranda's birthday.

On Presidents' Day, he is relieved that no one gives him a thought. They're out buying cars and major appliances. If, here and there, Lincoln's ghost and Washington's are roused in a cursory way, William Henry Harrison's is luckier: we leave him undisturbed, in dignity and peace.

There is a Harrison or a Harrisonburg in Arkansas, Georgia, Idaho,
    Louisiana, Michigan, Montana, Nebraska, New York, South Dakota, and
    Virginia. There is a Harrison Bay in Alaska. All of them may
    have been named for William Henry. Or some. Or, as he might
    have preferred, none.

There is a Mount Harrison on Mahé Island in the Indian Ocean. The chances
    that it has anything to do with William Henry Harrison are remote. But
    then so is Mahé Island.

The country he imagined in his inaugural address never existed, but that is
    where he would have been at home.

El Adon: A Piyyut

All his creation, El rules.
Blessed by whatever lives and breathes, he
completes with his goodness the world he rules,
dressed in his robes of wisdom and judgment—
El, the master of heaven's host. He shines
forth in his chariot's splendor, bright in his dazzling
garb so that Righteousness bends low and bows its
head, while Purity blushes and Kindness melts
in an earnest resolve to try to do even better.
Just as he made them, these bright Lights of the
Lord are good and they radiate wisdom and truth.
Mighty they are: their luster, eternal,
never can tarnish or dim, and they order the world
over which they radiate splendid auroras,
poured forth as hymns of praise and joy.
Quick to do their master's bidding, they give
respect to his holy name and glory that
shines as bright as the sun he summoned or
the moon he made for its answer in silver.
Untamed, the constellations howl their endless
variations of thanks and praise for his measureless greatness.

A Fable of Odo of Cheriton

The knight asks of a scholar what paradise
and its promised joys are like, and the scholar replies:
"Such as the eye has never seen or the ear
has never heard, or the heart of man felt here.
Such rare delights do heaven's angels prepare
that those who've loved God may be rewarded there."
"But are there hawks," the knight inquires, "and hounds?"
a question that almost goes beyond the bounds
of civil discourse. The scholar tells him, "No,
it is not fit for dogs to enter so
delightful a venue as heaven." Hearing this,
the knight confesses that his idea of bliss
would be somewhat diminished if the chase
were not a part of its perfection. Grace
should lead each to his own kind of delight.
The scholar then tells this story to the knight:
   A lion once prepared a feast
   to which he summoned every beast,
   a sumptuary banquet where
   there was on offer extravagant fare
   of every kind to impress and please
   the taste of every creature. These
   animals all fell to with zest,
   declaring each new course as best.
   At last, when the rich feast was done,
   they said goodnight and everyone
   headed happily home again.
   The wolf, on the way back to his den,
   chanced to encounter a pig he knew,
   gorging himself, as pigs will do,
   on garbage. He paused to say hello.
   The pig asked him, "Where do you go
   at such an hour, Sir Wolf?" to which
   the wolf replied he'd had a rich

repast with the lion. "Weren't you there?"
he asked. "We had amazing dishes,
dainties beyond one's wildest wishes!"
"Such lovely things on which to dine,
but did he offer what we swine
prefer?" the pig asked. The wolf was tired.
"What's that?" he nevertheless inquired.
"Garbage," the pig said. "Refuse. Swill."
"I don't understand. I never will,"
the wolf said and went home to sleep,
leaving the pig on his garbage heap.
Some men, the scholar then explains to the knight,
are like that pig: they wallow in filth, quite
content, even proud of the mire they're covered in
and they love the Lord less than they love their sin.

Poetry Reading

At the lectern in front of the room, the poet goes on
and on, full of himself and his own importance,
and full of the words he intones in a slow singsong.

My attention, my eyes wander around the room
where the audience sits, apparently attentive,
or at least polite, and I wonder at them, and about them . . .
But one in the right rear, his face upturned,
with his head fallen back that way and his mouth agape?
Asleep? Or perhaps dead?
Either way, he is lucky.

Anti-poem

Corrections, elaborations, refinements: we chatter,
even when we agree. I try to imagine

silence, as if in the woods where trees concur
entirely, stand at ease or sway in the wind

together as of one mind or no mind at all.
In that pine-needle tang, what is there to say

while their intricate shadows dapple the ground in the stillness,
a blessed concord where wise and stupid meet?

Fritillaries

The fluttering of the fritillary is . . . what?
Tutelary? Instructive: the liliaceous
plant with which it shares its name and to which
I like to think it might be attracted was called that
by Noel Capperon, an Orléans druggist,
because of its checkered leaves he thought resembled
a painted dice box—*fritillus* in Latin.
And the common fritillary—the plant, I mean,
the Guinea-hen flower, Turkey-hen flower, or sometimes
Pheasant or Leopard's Lily, or Checkered Lily,
or even the Checkered Daffodil—has indeed
a drooping dull red flower with pink and purple
squares and blotches. (Bees like it; butterflies,
not so much.) The Chinese use the bulbs
to make a tea for loosening phlegm, but avoid
the heart of the bulb which is poison (wouldn't you know?).
But, no, I wouldn't. This is all swotted from books,
while real learning comes from walking the woods,
spotting the plants, seeing the butterflies,
and recognizing that what I'm watching fly by
is not a Monarch, say, but a Variegated
Fritillary looking for nectar it likes
from the butterflyweed, common milkweed, dogbane,
peppermint, red clover, swamp milkweed,
and perhaps the tickseed sunflower—of which
I might know how to pick out maybe the milkweed.
There is also the Great Spangled Fritillary
that is partial to violets, and the Regal Fritillary,
endangered now . . . I've never seen one, or never
known if I did, which is worse. There are several others,
even in Massachusetts, whose names I write down,
Silver-bordered, Atlantis, and Aphrodite,
each of them pleasant enough to indict the flighty
inattention of misspent days and years

that seem to have been my life. Trees, birds, the flowers
underfoot, and the stars overhead I know
only as children do, but with less wonder.
Their names are words I ought to have been alert to . . .
The Niobe, the Queen of Spain Fritillary . . .
How could I not have responded to such sweet
blandishments, such fritiniency (the next
word in the lexicon, the chirping of locusts
or cicadas)? And butterflies, I'm pleased to say,
are prettier and blissfully, blessedly silent.

The Fire Eater: A Roundel

Inured but not insensible to pain,
the fire eater breathes flame into the air,
making by this a game of his despair.

Brave, is he? Reckless? Foolish? Or insane?
We cannot guess, not having, ourselves, been there.
       Inured but not insensible to pain,
       the fire eater breathes flame into the air.

He shows a body mastered by its brain
and asks us to admire what we can't bear,
who fear what he does not. (And do we dare?)
       Inured but not insensible to pain,
       the fire eater breathes flame into the air,
making by this a game of his despair.

Doodling

The pen is ever heavier in the hand,
which is also weaker. Also? The one could be

an obvious misperception caused by the other.
They are not, however, mutually exclusive.

All I know is that this seems harder to do,
and I promise myself that I'm only fooling around.

I remember—but only barely—when I believed
that fooling around wasn't only fooling around.

Doodling. It's one of those verbs that occurs
only in the frequentative. Like idle.

The time stretches out: the game is less and less fun
(or the time grows short: the game is less and less fun),

and the pen is ever heavier in the hand,
which is also, of course, and as I have said, weaker.

The Duke of Gornisht-Helfen

I

The waves racing onshore glint in the sun,
delightful to all but one, who sees how it is,
how they flee from the ocean, desperate, afraid of the water,
trying to climb the strand, and they fail and fall back,
and die.
         Does the Duke of Gornisht-Helfen share
this odd insight?
               No, for even if true,
it would only burden the others there on the beach.

2

He lives in his gate house now, his derelict palace
behind him. He never looks out in that direction.
Those windows are heavily draped. He'd rather remember,
or better yet, imagine, correcting defects,
repairing the roof, say, reopening wings,
and lighting again the torchères and chandeliers
as if for a grand ball.
              How does he bear it?
He shrugs and asks in reply, "But who is not
diminished? What man alive, of a certain age,
cannot remember a glorious past that is gone?
Such recollections are not an indictment." He pauses
to correct himself, "Or, anyway, not always."

3

"I am not myself, today." It's a common
locution of mild complaint, but there is another
logical possibility—a different
or even a better self.

But who believes
in any such transformations?
                    The Duke explains
that what we always mean is: we've been demoted,
are servants now to that overbearing self
who has taken to bed or isn't quite right in the head,
the tyrannical master of whom we'd rather steer clear,
but, as in Figaro's song of complaint, the bell
rings and we are obliged once more to respond.

        4

He used to go into the village incognito,
although all of us knew who he was. What the children's stories
never admit is the reason for these disguises,
which isn't to fool the populace, or discover
what they are thinking and saying about their lord
but would never say to his face. It is worse than that:
what the man in the almost perfect disguise wants
is escape for a while from himself, from that overbearing
master up on the hill. And if he discovered
there were some plot against him, he'd want to join it.

        5

The park, of course, has run wild, or rather say
that its shrubs and trees have taken over. Rousseau's
imperative, that each of us be authentic
and true to some inner nature, is here on display.
The plants, of course, have no imagination
and cannot understand the idea of a garden.
They do what they do, and each week are worse than before,
in a steady declension for which one develops a taste
and a talent—a doctor's knack of precise observation.

The range of his walks increases: in overgrown
pathways, the palace is hidden. Those sweeping vistas
he remembers from his youth are no longer congenial
and gradually, tactfully, disappear.

6

Liberty, they want, and equality,
as if those were both possible together.
(But you cannot try to reason with a mob,
even if it's only a single person.)
The Duke, nevertheless, finds their ambitions
interesting—he never had any, himself.
To what can the eldest son of a duke aspire?
Majority and the death of a father will come
inevitably and one will assume the title.
Or burden, although not heavy. But, anyway, fate.
He used to make a joke—that one may shed
but cannot deny his blood. Now he just shrugs
and says, instead, that what we discover in life
is how to accept that entropy is a friend.

Rondeau

Flailing in a pit of woe,
I groan and let the whole world know
my suffering, and I make plain
the brutal truth of my great pain.
I do this in a French rondeau.

A useless game this is, although
diverting, even soothing, so
distracting as I wrack my brain
for rhymes are hard to find.

And anodyne, for there's a slow
returning to the status quo
ante: I feel myself regain
some equanimity. Right as rain?
Not by any means. Oh, no,
I've not yet lost my mind.

A Cat's Life

Her repertoire is limited but fulfilling,
with two preoccupations, or three, perhaps,
if you include the taking of many naps:
otherwise she is snuggling or killing.

Suits

Each morning, as I confront my closet's array,
I have to admit again that the life I lead
is hardly good enough: I have not been named
ambassador to Malta; I am not on the board

of any college or large corporation; I shall not
receive a major prize today and pose
for photographers. Those suits, the shirts, the ties
are ready, but I am not, and the shoes are shined

as they wait for different occasions than I imagined
on the tailor's block, when I shopped for a dandified
future brighter than what I expect or deserve.
Even for weddings and funerals that require
a suit, I choose from the second best, reserving
that one for the dream into which I yet hope to awake.

In the Playground

We are boisterous children playing out in a field
with a ball we can hardly see in a gathering darkness;
now and again, we hear our mothers calling
and wander off, some of us, good little boys
and girls, responding promptly, while others, reluctant,
dawdle and try to defy at least for a while
the obvious fact that the circle of those remaining
to catch an increasingly ghostly ball is smaller,
and ignore the hard question of which is worse,
to be the last to leave, or the next to last.

When in Rome

Not to be mere museum, and not to allow us
to relax, relapse to tourists and connoisseurs,
its traffic, first of all, sordid, aggressive,

lets us know, time after time, how timing
is everything—you could get killed. There needn't be
lions inside that floodlit ruin: Peugeots'

grilles sport rampant beasts as ravenous. We
adjust and learn to make our way, to church
and gallery, shunning what poses for travel brochures

in our quest for something special, refined. And here
the Roman gods look down with their ancient wisdom
to provide the instruction visitors always require,

on the Spanish Steps, perhaps, or the Termini Station,
where there are not only beggars whenever you need one
(whether you know it or not) but even thieves.

Panic Attack

I

Suppose they are right after all, that the honors, jobs,
and the shabby glamour they have so long withheld
were all along beyond my poor deserving.

I do, sometimes, but go anyway, to confront
them, who may in their comfy chairs, so richly
endowed, entertain reciprocal doubts, even wonder

whether they owe it all to the fickle lady.
But I can't suppose. I am not, after all, the performer,
and no one is paying me any attention—the point

of the game. In which sad case I can relax,
and perhaps let the young man I used to be,
the invalid within, that innocent, listen.

2

Rilke? Roethke? Whoever it was who said,
"You must change your life," was being too easy. What then?
The indifference one learns to live with, but crude affronts

and humiliations call forth some self-protective
adaptations: a reciprocal indifference?
a lively arrogance? numbness? Which have, as we learn,

their own defects. And each of them comes with costs.
I can feel on the back of my neck the hostile eyes
of those who have done me wrong, and therefore despise me.

My father was right about law school. And Tolstoy was right:
making shoes is useful, honest work.
You must change your life again. And then again.

3

Acute remarks, or even cute remarks
won from my parents' ambition and love, the praise
to which one becomes addicted. Poetry mimics

those happy moments, but slowly. Poetry readings
in real time and face to face enact
those all but forgotten moments just closely enough

so that we are half aware of what's always missing.
L'esprit de l'escalier, but it's they who've ascended
that elegant and endless spiral stairway

from which, at moments, we can persuade ourselves
we hear faint echoes of loving, approving laughter.
If poetry ever aspires, it is to that.

4

An image persists or a cadence, and days have gone by
to dull the ache and prove the odd phrase's value.
Do I bother? Better ask which bothers more,

to revert to my bad habit or try to fight it?
I do what I know how to do, and for some few minutes
bask in that approval, forever gone

except in what remains of my yearning. The spirit
tires, sickens, inviting the dumb body
to follow on that tempting downhill path,

but along the way, fall flowers, glints of sunshine
on water I know is bone-chilling cold, and fleecy
clouds in the sky, demand that one take notice.

Parmenion: On the Epigram

Greek Anthology IX.342

An epigram that goes on for too many lines
affronts the Muses' laws and just designs:
stamina is for marathon runners, but speed—
of the sprint or dash—is what makers of epigrams need.

Flyover Country

From a height where no bird soars, those whorls, meanders,
and curlicues of hillsides, rivers, and shorelines
suffer or, say, deplore our impositions,
the roadways and boundary lines our labors impose.
They coexist but uneasily, contradicting
each another, the round and straight, and in their slow,
relentless dispute, the eventual winner is clear,
for what the winds and rains cannot themselves

obliterate, the earth in its drowse shrugs off.
From my window seat, as I follow a highway incised
on the plain below, such a brave and hopeless thing,
I stare at the crazed lines on the palm of my hand
and think of the brain's involutions in dumb wonder,
looking down, at what our minds and hands have done.

Ctimene

Homer mentions her only once: the swineherd
alludes to "Ctimene of the flowing gowns,"
Anticlea's daughter, Odysseus' younger sister,
of whom he has thought for those long years of the war
and the years of the homeward journey, so far as we're told,
not even once. But she, we may suppose,
has thought of him, while Penelope's loutish suitors
swarmed about and her nephew Telemachus grew,
and with whatever combination of pity, concern,
resentment, and love, we may, as our temperaments prompt,
supply. Ctimene married, the herdsman tells
Odysseus, a Samian prince who brought dower gifts
and took her away, the one who had shared his childhood,
lived in their house, breathed the same air, and knew
the look of the hills and sky in all weathers and seasons.
What his home-sickness all that time had yearned for,
she had known too and yearned for as well, and her brother,
the one who could prove it had not been merely a dream.

Stress

Because birdsong is such an intricate behavior, it may be a sensitive
indicator of a male's fitness. Producing a song is a difficult task for
the brain, and any additional challenge—lack of food, infections, or
other types of stress—is likely to take a toll.
    —Clive Catchpole, University of London

The appeal to nature is dangerous, but we cannot
therefore ignore it altogether. Consider
the sparrows Nowicki and Searcy had fed, as much
as they wanted: they flourished and learned to perform their songs

correctly. But we are not just talking art.
It is procreation, repeating the genes, for the females
demand precision, a sign of health if not
of cultivation and taste. The birds they'd fed less

learned the songs less well, achieving an average
sixteen syllables right of a possible twenty.
(They were also somewhat smaller and often weaker.)
Their twitterings, imperfect and less than accomplished,

won them fewer offers of copulation,
and the females, the theory goes, were right to be picky,
wanting to mate with the best and the strongest. The lesson
for poets? It's what we knew all along, that stress

and deprivation, however melodramatic,
and even appealing—think of those dreadful lives
we read about of Mandelstam, or Célan,
or Rimbaud—cannot compare with classical training,

proper tuition, and uninterrupted practice.
Our hearts may not go out to these creatures of comfort,
children of Mandarin privilege, unacquainted
with the urgent woes of our time. But they've learned how to sing.

Birthday Poems

68

My age, I tell myself, is a passing grade,
but "passing," takes on a different meaning now
from what schoolchildren worry about. The number
is a sensible thermostat setting or good golf score,

but the years will heat the one past the comfort range
and nibble away at the other so no handicap—
and there will be ever greater handicaps—
can compensate. And what can one do but play through?

69

This is the last of the years in the Bible's promise,
but there was no warranty, and infants can die
as well or badly as anyone else. The number
is startling, sobering, nevertheless. What I face

next year is clearly senescence: the promise has been
fulfilled, and will be fulfilled. Our library books
come due whether or not we have read them through
or understood them. It is all borrowed time.

70

I enter the grim decade from which neither parent
emerged, although that doesn't mean I won't.
My life has been easier, luckier than theirs,
which is what they wanted for me and would still want.

But they don't get to choose, nor do I, and the prospect
dims and clarifies. I can sometimes manage
indifference, but, like faith, that comes and goes,
and all I have left to fall back on is good manners.

Chicago Art Institute, after Lunch

Not the foreshortened ice-cream cone as it first
seemed but a "Glass of Beer," 1914,
by Juan Gris. Yes, I see it now, and my thirst
was slaked not ten minutes ago with the cold clean

taste of a beer that I hadn't, it now appears,
appreciated sufficiently. The small
pleasures of life that, over the course of years
one comes to take for granted . . . These are all

there is, as these artists testify: fruit, flowers,
a view of a field or mountain, a striking face.
What more could one want or need? The painters' powers
recall to us these occasions of special grace.

Primary Grades

It is only by some unruly misreading that I
can indulge myself and suppose that their purpose, unknown
of course to them, was to teach me these difficult lessons
in how to endure benign neglect. My classmates'
names I cannot remember, and even the teachers'
are fading: Miss Jennings, Miss Wood, Miss Stolle, Miss—
or was it Mrs.?—Conklin, Miss Peck ... None
liked me much, or thought I was bright. But how could they
have known? Intelligence, talent, or even their promise,
all of which looked like impertinence to them,
were not what they knew how to value or recognize.
But they do not have the last word, and one may imagine
some insect that fertilizes a rare plant
and enables its survival. The insect's intention
has nothing to do with the large, pale, and almost
odorless blossom that later on appears,
months, even years after the bug has died.

Collected Poems

These books of poems are lives, which is why we turn
first, as in biographies too, to the death,
to see what the plot was and how it came out.
I've noticed that this is what I do these days.
It's a recent taste, opening volumes of verse
as if I were reading their Hebrew texts that God
may still prefer. What had the poet learned
of the craft or of life? What wisdom or folly informed

those lines he set down? And God's generous vision
and hopes are mine for the moment: who would not welcome
excellence, strength, and truth? Selfish, I wish
for a crowning, not to say redeeming, grace
to which the life and whole body of work
in a not so serendipitous way were tending.

Monticore

That Roy Horn should be mauled by Monticore,
his 600-pound white tiger, out there in Vegas,
on the Mirage stage on a Friday night turns
the act less silly, abruptly redeeming the sequins,
the cheap music, the show-biz props, and the lights,
for it proves what we all but forgot—that the danger is real,
and the taming of brute nature never secure.
Daniel did it, but only that one time:
Siegfried and Roy turned it into a business
with a cast and crew of 267,
and they had a lifetime contract . . . (But what good is that
if you risk your life every night?) It seized Roy's arm
in its jaws, he struck the beast with a microphone,
and then the tiger grabbed his neck and dragged him
offstage.
          Siegfried came out at length to announce
the performance was cancelled. Or was it rather perfected,
what people had come to see? That the strength of Daniel's
virtue should offer protection must seem, in Vegas,
miraculous, where prayers at the tables and wheels,
however venal, are fervent enough. Even there,
the Lord can keep us safe, whose infinite mercy
is not a mirage, for our sins are infinite, too.
Drum roll, fanfare, spotlight. We hang in the balance.

Attention

On my daughter-in-law's refrigerator door,
a magnet offers Talmudic cheer, or comfort,
with news of the angel over each blade of grass,
whispering, "Live! Live!"
                              But angels are flighty,
too easily distracted, and grass turns brown,
having perhaps relied too much on heaven.

One cannot argue with angels, who do their best.
Attention, itself, is the problem, I fear, that sudden
coming clear of perception, purpose, interest,
for a while only, and then it blurs and fades.
But I cannot be rude to my angel: he's old and tired
and doesn't see so well anymore. I tell him
that he can still do it and that I have faith,
but belief fades too, as I know he knows.

Bus

Nothing has changed: the familiar street remains
what it was, a welter of random traffic, until
you position yourself at the corner beneath a sign

and stare—how can you not?—the two or three blocks
of your field of vision to try to make out the white
roof of the bus that ought any minute to be

appearing in the middle distance. That mere
looking imposes an order. The cars, the trucks,
the taxis are all not-bus, and the bus you want,

withholding itself, teasing, defying, looms
in its invisibility larger than buses should.
So it can be with dawn, or the mailman, the waiter,

or, for that matter, the heaven we dream of, waiting,
with its warmth and lights, bearing down through the distance and time
it and your yearning shape and almost tame.

The Ghost in the Corner

When I visit my children these days, a ghost attends me,
not my mother's, not anymore, but my own,
a novice, an almost undetectable presence,
diffident, say, that lurks in a corner, observing,

getting to know the rooms in which it will visit,
and offering only now and again suggestions—
for its benefit, surely, more than my own—
that I might be more amusing, cheerful, attentive,

to leave a better impression, to make those calls
to which it looks forward more pleasant on both sides.
Are my sons unaware? Has my daughter never noticed
or felt its moods of affection and resignation?
Or has he introduced himself and whispered
on my behalf, as if I were already gone?

Santa Clara Pot

Uselessness is what it proclaims: it cannot
even hold water, would melt at such a chore.

What it does contain is purer, the idea of water,
the shape water might take, its aspiration.

That black luster is legacy of a fire
fueled by horseshit. (What else in that desert burns?)

And fragile? As any crystal or fine china,
it demands our attention—love!—in the absence of which

it threatens to shed its perfection and, in a moment,
revert, to punish our faithlessness, to mud.

On Circe's Island

From that magic place where men can turn into beasts,
and Odysseus has to choose, resisting temptation,
to leave the comforts, the luxuries she offers,
and resume his homeward journey, the only route
leads through Ocean's furthest reaches to Hades'
ever-gloomy shore: or in plain language,
a man must die to be born again. On the island,
what blandishments were there, beyond the details
Homer mentions, the gold and silver vessels,
chairs with silver nails, the linens, the rich
hangings, the carpeted bedchamber . . . ?

                                        Deep in the park,
I imagine a kind of gazebo, a study house,
and a bearded Jew, a rabbi, who looks up
from the scrolls on his reading table to welcome the Greek,
and together they discuss the idea of exile,
which is what they both know so well, and the yearning for home,
that dream one may try to realize. Or not.
"Ithaca?" he asks. "It will have changed,
for life has gone on. And what you are likely to find
will break your heart."

                         "Hearts are made to be broken,"
is how Odysseus answers. The rabbi nods,
acknowledging, if not quite agreeing.

                                 "But exile?
This is the human condition. From Eden, first.
But from childhood, too, and our mothers' arms. We become
whatever has happened to us. This, now, is our nature
as well as our plight."

                           "If we give in, it is,"
the Greek replies, and they sit together in silence.

We know what happens: both, in the end, go home,
to learn what neither, however wise or crafty,
ever imagined—that a man can go home again
to learn in his well-timbered halls nostalgia
for the island, strange and sometimes lovely, of exile.

Adventure

Every day, on trivial errands, I face
terrible carnage, bent metal, blood, the appalled
stares of passers-by . . . I needed mixed nuts,
something to serve with drinks, and it was hot,
so why walk the few blocks? That is what cars
are for, for heaven's sake. But heaven is watching,
its malign eye eager for any such chance.
In the smash-up, I'm dying, again as I often do,
and watch in the horror I share with the crowd of strangers.
But does that stop me? No, one must be brave,
reckless even. . . . . If blood is the price of warfare,
then of mixed nuts, too, the chores of life, its demands
before which we'll never surrender. I have confronted
as bad or worse twenty times this week, and somehow
press forward still, attack, attack, attack,
and despite the odds I make it, arrive at the store,
and manage to get back home in time for the guests,
my friends, to whom I will not for pride's sake
admit my fears or allude to catastrophes
I have evaded once more, but only just.

Complexity

What makes things baffling is their degree of complexity,
not their sheer size. . . . a star is simpler than an insect.
—Martin Rees, Astronomer Royal

If there were just the one star, that might be true,
but as astrophysicists know, there are lots of them out there,
and how they move, and where they came from and where
they're going becomes sufficiently complex
to keep one occupied. Do the stars portend?
Do zodiacal signs not signify? Can a nova
bright in the winter sky lead the three kings
to a spot where something has happened? Or, changing focus,

we wonder how long our mother sun will continue
to shine and fend off the limitless cold and silent
darkness—or, now, it turns out, not so silent:
there's a black hole in the Perseus galaxy cluster
giving off a B flat, 87 octaves
below middle C, like the buzz of a huge horsefly.

Scab

A part of my body, of me, but then somehow,
because of whatever happened, internal strife
or trauma from outside, it seceded, withdrew,
breaking its bonds with the rest of me and my life
to become something else, estranged, and in this new
relationship strike out, independent now.

The change is subtle. At first, I am unaware
of anything different, though messages from those
nerves no longer arrive. But then the nearby
tissue has some sense of loss: it knows
and wants me to know that something has gone awry.
I sense an itch, an irritation there

and also an annoyance I cannot ignore,
as in family quarrels and civil wars, where each
party is aggrieved and feels betrayed.
"Don't pick at it," my mother used to teach,
"it'll get infected." I knew but disobeyed,
picked at the scab, and left an angry sore

that, nevertheless, was entirely me and mine.
Its redness would subside, and even the itch,
the last reminder of what had happened, would fade.
I never supposed there was any question which
was me and which was not, but I am afraid
that there will come a time when that clear line

blurs, and I depart, leaving behind
a corpse that is, in effect, an enormous scab
I've picked at and managed at last to tear away.
It won't be myself laid out there on a slab
but something utterly foreign that, one day,
my soul sloughed off, the body and the mind.

Thirteen Ways of Looking at Robert Lowell

1

We are walking past one another, and he sees me,
knows me, and knows that I know who he is.
But he dislikes me, having treated me badly,
having voted against me for some grant.
He knows that I know this.
He sees me affect not to see him.
He pretends not to see me either.
We pass on Mt. Auburn Street
like the two strangers each of us wishes we were.

2

He has no idea who I am.
He is out of his mind,
as he often was, full of himself or full
of his mad thoughts. (He kept trying to call
Jackie Onassis, thinking that he and she
were right for each other.)
He does not see the hatred in my eyes,
or my eyes, or me,
as we pass one another on Mt. Auburn Street
on the Signet Club Corner.

3

He sees me. I see him.
We are each convinced the other is a piece of shit.
He looks up at the sky. I look down at the ground.
Should I punch him in the mouth?
Yes, but I don't.
He's flabby, and he shambles, but he's big.
And maybe, in prison, he learned how to fight.

4

What could I have said to the eminent poet?
That it's a shame they put in the parking garage
under the Boston Common,
and it's a terrible shame that they moved the aquarium.
And your poem, mourning these tragic events . . .
It's a joke, right?
All this within a step or two
on a pleasant afternoon on Mt. Auburn Street.

5

A. J. Liebling was married to Jean Stafford,
the first wife of Robert Lowell,
who later married Elizabeth Hardwick,
who wanted to be Mary McCarthy,
who was married to Edmund Wilson,
who looked a little like A. J. Liebling.

And you, sir, are the weakest
link in this daisy chain.

6

Of course it doesn't talk.
It is an enormous dummy
operated by Frank Bidart,
the Edgar Bergen of American Poetry.
But at this particular moment
on a fall afternoon on Mt. Auburn Street,
there is no ventriloquist.
There's just Robert Lowell and me.

7

I'd met him once before,
in his apartment in New York,
reporting some story or other for *Newsweek*.
I didn't hate him then, but I didn't like him either.
Like many loonies, he must have managed to sense this,
and feeling threatened, he hated me
and was convinced that he was hating me back.

8

"You're Robert Lowell," I say accusingly
as we pass each other there on Mt. Auburn Street.
"Why did you do that to me, you son of a bitch?"
His eyes go wide; he's embarrassed.
No, he's terrified.
He doesn't answer in words
but makes high squeaky noises, like a mewing cat.

Or, no, that was George Starbuck on the telephone,
not explaining to me why he couldn't hire me at B. U.
But it doesn't matter. Both of them are dead.

9

Lowell died in a taxicab in New York
on the way from the airport into Manhattan.
He had a massive coronary.
That could have happened years earlier
on that pleasant afternoon on Mt. Auburn Street
just as we were passing each other,
and I could have stopped and looked down
and not offered to help.

10

I suppose as we passed each other that day,
I could have said something to the eminent poet,
but what was there to say?
Something witty but wounding,
something superior.
"Hey, Cal!" (I never called him Cal.)
"You know it wasn't panettone that your mother's corpse was like,
wrapped in tinfoil.
It was panforte.
Or maybe a suppository!"
I prefer the line like that.
And it's one of his best lines.

11

He was a jerk, a son of a bitch, a total disaster,
but as I passed him that day on Mt. Auburn Street,
I thought, Jim Dickey is even worse.
But I like Jim Dickey better.

12

Talent? I guess,
but as much for self-promotion as for poetry.
His success, his jobs at Harvard and at B. U.,
his deal with Farrar, Straus that kept bringing out
different versions of the same not very wonderful book . . .
I don't envy any of that,
and if he had offered that day, there on Mt. Auburn Street
to trade places with me, to swap lives,
I'd have refused.
He was miserable and crazy, and he's dead.
And I am alive. And while not many people know it,
I am the better poet.

13

I am there on Mt. Auburn Street,
but on a whim I turn off to go up Dunster
to La Flamme, to see George, for a haircut.
Lowell needs a haircut. He always needed a haircut,
but he's not good at grooming, and he doesn't stop.
So we miss each other.

Just. But enough.

One-Word Poem

Motherless.

DISCUSSION QUESTIONS:

1. Is this a joke? And, if so, is it a joke of the poet in which the editor of the magazine (or, later, the book publisher or the textbook writers) has conspired? Or is it a joke *on* the editors and publishers? Is the reader the audience of the poem?

2. It is regrettable not to have a mother. Is the purpose of the poem to convey an emotion to the reader? Does the poet suppose that this is the saddest word in the language? Do you agree or disagree? Can you suggest a sadder word?

3. The Supplement to the *Oxford English Dictionary* gives an alternate meaning from nineteenth- and twentieth-century Australian slang as an intensifier, as in "stone motherless broke." Can you assume that the poet knew this? Does this make for an ambiguity in the poem? Does this information change your emotional response?

4. If the assertion of the single word as a work of art is not a joke, then what could it mean? Is it a Dada-ist gesture, amusing and cheeky perhaps but with an underlying seriousness that the poet either invites or defies the reader to understand?

5. Even if the poet was merely fooling around, does that necessarily diminish the possible seriousness of the poem?

6. If we acknowledge that this is a work of art, can the author assert ownership? Is it possible to copyright a one-word poem?

7. In writing a one-word poem, the crucial decision must be which word to choose and to posit as a work of art. Do you think the poet spent a great deal of time picking this word? Or did he simply open a dictionary and let his fingers do the walking? Does that diminish the poem's value? Or is it a kind of bibliomancy?

8. Should the word have been in quotes? Or is it quotes even without being in quotes? There is a period at the end of the poem. Would it change the meaning of the poem if there were an exclamation point? Or no punctuation at all? Would that be a different poem? Better or worse? Or would you like it more or less? (Are these different questions?)

9. You can almost certainly write—or "write"—a one-word poem. But it would be difficult for you to get it published—almost certainly more difficult now that this one has been published and staked its claim. Is the publication of a poem a part of the creative act? Had the poet written his poem and put it away in his desk drawer as Emily Dickinson used to do, would this make it a different poem?

10. Some poems we read and some that we particularly like, we memorize. You have already memorized this one. Do you like it better now? Or are the questions part of the poem, so that you have not yet memorized it? Will you, anyway? Do you need to memorize the questions verbatim, or is the idea enough?

Poem without Even One Word

DISCUSSION QUESTIONS:

1. This, too, must be a joke. But it depends at least in part on the previous poem. If a poem can have only one word, why can't there be a poem without any words at all? Can there be a significant silence? Is this part of the point of this poem?

2. Prompted as we are to think of the previous poem, can we assume that "Motherless" has faded, and that this poem is about—or is a demonstration of, or re-enactment of—the mourning process and the extinction of grief?

3. It could, of course, as easily be about the sheer incomprehensibility of experience. Or writer's block. Or the uselessness of poetry in the face of pain and death. Which would you prefer?

4. It could also be an attempt further to discommode the editors and readers of poetry, for if the author can assert that the one-word poem is a poem, then why ought not he to press his advantage and assert that even this wordlessness is a poem, if he says so. Do we admire or deplore this demonstration of power?

5. John Cage had a famous performance piece in which he came out, sat at the piano for 4 minutes and 33 seconds, and then, without having played a single note, got up and left the stage. It was either a composition entirely of rests, or it was a way of directing the attention of the audience to the ambient and accidental sounds in the hall, or it was a joke. Or all three. Could the Cage work be the "music" for this "poem"? Compare and contrast this silence with that.

6. Robert Rauschenberg has a work in the San Francisco Museum of Art which is an erasure of a de Kooning drawing. One can see faint remains of the original drawing—or persuade oneself that he does. Bakunin said that "to destroy is also a creative act." Discuss.

7. The only way to "erase" this poem would be to put a word in the blank space. Do you feel invited to do this? Or dared? Are you flattered or offended by this possibility of collaboration?

8. The overwhelming likelihood these days is that an encounter with a poem will be in a classroom setting. Few people read poems for pleasure now. (Not even teachers of poetry are readers of poetry.) In this peculiar environment,

poems survive not "in the wild" but in the zoo-like setting of the academy where short poems are preferred because there is less time spent on the poem itself and more on the explication and discussion. In such circumstance, is this not the ideal poem? Could this become your favorite poem? And if that happened, would that make you a connoisseur or a barbarian?

9. To study poems in a classroom is to pervert them and put them to uses for which they were never intended, but a wordless poem is less likely to be damaged than any other. Is this, then, a poem of protest?

10. Frame your own question, making it as provocative and enlivening as you can, and add it here.

French Postcards

Oui, si yeux oie rire!

꧁

I am sending you this postcard. It is not of Paris, although it is from Paris. It is of me, or of us, for as I write, I imagine you reading these words, just as I suppose you, while reading them, might well be imagining me,
writing them.

Ah, yes, you see it now, don't you? Wish you were here!

How silly!

But what would be the rationale of a serious postcard?

You could be imagining me imagining you as I am imagining you imagining me . . .

That is by the bye.

Bye.

꧁

This is the text of the postcard. It is in a foreign language here. The photo on the other side is of a native scene. There will be a time when these qualities will reverse themselves, changing places so that, when you receive this, the text will be native and the picture foreign.

There is a kind of sadness to such faithlessness.

Faithfully yours,

꧁

Actually, this is a postcard of itself, as all postcards are. I mean by this only that there are others, its brothers, on the rack. The card is self-referential in another way, for if you were to burn the postcard you would have to remember it as something gone, which it was, for me, as soon as I mailed it. Only then would your postcard and mine be the same again.

And tomorrow, if I were to send you another, it would be a souvenir of this one.

But I won't, because you would have to burn that one, too.

✺

"This is not a postcard."

—René Magritte

(But it does require a stamp.)

✺

They say that the light is different here in Paris. I suppose it may be, but then all light is the same, is it not? A wave and yet also a particle?

(M. d'Onde, that would be.)

If you burn this postcard, too, you will see it in a new light, a Parisian light, from Parisian fuel.

Or will that, too, have gone native?

✺

The picture on a postcard is unimportant.

The words on a postcard do not signify.

The signature is all.

(Unsigned)

✺

If the postcards' pictures are unimportant, how do I choose? Shall I indulge myself, picking the least attractive card because I feel sorry for it? Can I suppose that the recipient will share this exquisite pity, so that through its banality or even ugliness we shall have conspired to make something quite original and even, in a small way, beautiful?

Surely, this is asking too much.

✺

"A strong misreading is the equivalent of a new postcard."

—Harold Bloom

(But does it then require a new stamp?)

✺

In shops, the racks of postcards are frequently near the door. Which is putting *des cartes* before *dehors*.

Causerie

— *Je veux des cartes?*

— You wish Descartes?

— I wish Descartes well.

— You wish a Cartesian well?

— Yes, I wish for a Cartesian well because Descartes was a deep thinker and Cartesian wells are deep. With still waters.

There are in Paris people who sell postcards of elsewhere. Of Stillwater, Oklahoma, par exemple.

Would Magritte have sent one of these?

A vigne eau en d'oeuf ultime.

Yes, the time we are having here is quite wonderful. But gone. This card is a souvenir, perhaps, not only of this time but of this space.

Or this matter in this space at this time.

If only I had more energy.

Your relative,

A. Einstein

If Philip Glass were without sin, he could first cast Einstein.

But in the Glass house, would that be a good idea?

This is our house, or, anyway, our hotel. An *X* marks the window that the real window does not, of course, have.

Or any letter at all, actually. Only this ridiculous postcard.

⟨⟩

Do I buy the same card for each of my friends? Or a variety of cards, which I would then have to allot?

(On what principle, pray?)

I could, of course, pray, which is to say, leave it to the gods and do it at random. How is this to be achieved?

Ah! Face down, I shuffle and deal the cards. Face down, I write the greetings and the addresses. Only then do I turn over the card to see which scene which friend will receive.

But would not all my friends be displeased to know of this rather impersonal system?

Can I keep a secret?

⟨⟩

The life of a postcard is brutally brief. At one end, it waits patiently in its bracket on the rack for the cruelly hovering hand of the purchaser to light and, at last, choose it. Then, it receives its message, its address, its stamp, and goes on its way to the recipient who will glance at it for a few seconds, perhaps show it to a husband or wife, and then, more probably than not, discard it.

⟨⟩

In disgust, perhaps, because what the card says is that I am thinking of you, but not enough to warrant a real present. A postcard is not a scarf, a charm, a *garniture de bureau*, or, indeed, even a demitasse spoon or tee shirt.

A tricky business, this.

⟨⟩

Let us, however, assume a card with a prominent recipient. Or a prominent sender. Or, better, both:

"Dear Hem—Having a wonderful time. And here you are! Love, Zelda and Scott"

The postcard shows a rosy-assed baboon grinning.

That makes it to the display case of The Prominent Library of Your Leading University, which is what one may call Postcard Heaven.

✣

Now, of course, Scott and Hem are, themselves monuments and
therefore postcards, and their faces are gazing out from the rack next to
the representations of the Eiffel Tower, the Pont Neuf, and Notre Dame.

✣

In our street and all through Paris, there are little plaques announcing
historical associations. Here died J. F. Huysman. In this hotel, Jean Giono used
to stay. Down the rue du Cherche Midi, there used to be a military prison in
which Captain Dreyfus was incarcerated. Also there was Rochambeau's house,
and that of Pierre Lafue.

(Who was he? Are there prank plaque-makers putting up disinformational
markers?)

✣

There should, of course, be postcards of these things, but sold only in the
relevant spots. It might not make much economic sense, but, aesthetically, his-
torically, and even personally, it would be much nicer to send or receive one of
these cards. Who would not feel a small quiver of pleasure at my assuming that,
of course, he would know all about Lafue, and be interested to know that he
lived just down the street from my hotel?

Imagine that!

(Which is, always, the object of the exercise.)

✣

We are across the street from the Museum Hébert, which is devoted
to the work of Ernest Hébert, a formal painter of the Second Empire. The mu-
seum might have postcards. Next door to it is the Ambassade de Mali, which is
not likely to sell souvenirs of any kind.

But could.

Postcards of Bamako monuments? Bumper stickers with the flag of
Mali and the slogan: "Not a joke country!"

⟡

I imagine the sad Malinese, discussing how, even though they are in Paris, their thoughts are of home:

On y soit qui à Mali pense.

⟡

Could there, perhaps, be photographs of that missionary who first translated the Gospels into fourteen of the thirty tribal languages of Mali, the great Pierre Lafue?

Having rendered the good news into Bambara, Bobo Fing, Bomu, Bozo (Hainyaxo), Bozo (Sorogama), Bozo (Tièma Cièwè), Bozo (Tiéyaxo), Dausahaq, Dogon, Duun, Fulbe Jeeri, Fulfulde (Maasina), Fuuta Jalon, and Jo, he was working on Jula, dictating from his deathbed. Or that was what his disciples believed, who faithfully transcribed each syllable he uttered. That the recitation turned out, alas, to be nothing more than the fevered and delirious raving of a dying man only adds, I think, to the grandeur of scene.

It would have been a perfect subject for one of Hébert's canvases.

⟡

Upstairs, in a couple of rooms of the Mali Embassy (or, for all I know, in a closet) is the Embassy of Benin. Also, I rather suspect, without postcards.

⟡

The postcard is at the intersection of the generic with the personal. Like a greeting card, it is printed, but there is space for an individual message. The French postcard—the old-fashioned "dirty postcard"—is now obsolete, I expect. When any Kansas village has its video store with a porno section, it is not so hard to keep 'em down on the farm after they've seen Paree.

What more can Paris show them?

Still, there was something charming about those old cards. No one could mail them home, because the customs inspectors and the postal authorities would have intervened. One was therefore buying a souvenir not of a place but a state of mind, and it could be sent not to any real address back home but only to a realm of sensuality and license, the address of which one could not even begin to imagine.

✺

The aristocrats of postcards, I suppose, must be those in the museum shops. What an elegant alternative to the Arch of Triumph is the Matisse cut-out of a blue nude . . .

Or is it? Our recipient has seen the Arch of Triumph, of course, but he has seen the Matisse, too, hasn't he?

And the scale is wrong. It's too small. The Modigliani's colors are off. The Corot seems not quite in register (but with Corot, how can one be sure?).

Anyway, there is something offensive about the turning of works of art into souvenirs. Was this what Matisse had in mind?

(Warhol, very likely, but Matisse?)

Our recipient may not be so scrupulous.

But how can we know this? And can we risk insulting him?

✺

Perhaps a painting less well known, or by an artist who is less well known. A picture not too appealing, one which could only appeal to a refined or even slightly bored sensibility. The recipient will have to be flattered by the compliment that is clearly implied.

But too clearly, which would be condescending?

Or not clearly enough, which would miss the point?

✺

I am inclined, therefore, to modest cards that are not images of paintings or even sculptures but representations of handicrafts. A Japanese kimono, perhaps, or a brass candlestick of an interesting shape.

Admittedly, these are not ideal as emblems of Paris, but they are safe, even with a recipient as fastidious as myself.

✺

"Here's looking at you, kid. (As of course, you are looking at here.)"

✺

Better than a postcard of the Poussin, for instance, there is a slide. But a slide is not a postcard and belongs, therefore, to another category. It is a gift.

If a slide of the Poussin is good, might not a book be better, or a tie? An Hermès wallet?

Trop cher!

That is, the gift is too cher, or the recipient is not cher enough.

❧

A picture of an altogether featureless wall!

Ah, but the wall is part of the Hotel de Quelconque, built for Madame de Louche by Louis enième. She lived here only eleven months and then, when her conspiracy with the cardinal was discovered, was forced to flee to Sweden where she died in poverty and obscurity. The Hotel became a convent for the Carmelites Without Shoes, most of whom were killed in the courtyard (one star). The building was then used as a prison, an archive for the department of bridges, roads, and windmills, a lycée, and, in 1942–44, by the Germans for the Bureau of Entertainments of Social Services of the Gestapo.

The sixteenth century boiseries have been entirely destroyed.

Wish you were here.

❧

The postcard, for all its awkwardness, is preferable to the camera, by which tourists turn themselves into their own Boswells. (Nothing wrong with this, in theory, but they have to be Dr. Johnsons to begin with.) The photographer's impulse is to capture the moment and hold onto the experience but the paradoxical result is that they lose the moment, displacing the reality of the experience from this quai in this breeze in this light to a living-room slide-show in East Orange (par exemple).

Logically, it compounds, in that while hubby photographs the gracious bow of the living statue near the Church of St. Germain dès Pres, wifey, with a camcorder, is getting the larger picture—his approach, his putting the franc in the hat on the pavement, his aiming of the Minolta, the bow of the statue, the resumption of the pose.

It's all there, all captured, but in their attempts to do so, they have missed it, were hardly there at all.

❧

— But there aren't postcards of the white-faced sheet-clad living statue, are there?

— No, but one can remember him. Indeed, how can one not, with that bead of sweat growing at the end of his nose? A demanding métier!

— Being a living statue?

— Living.

❧

The two actions need not be linked, however, and the purchase of a postcard without any particular recipient in mind is not an inherently tainted gesture. One picks up odd and interesting cards at particular occasions. I bought a couple of such cards today at the Limoges exposition at the Petit Luxembourg. One shows a 1922 salière in the form of a cocotte, or casserole. (Actually, it looks like a small origami chicken worked in porcelain.) The other is a coupelle, a saucer-like rimmed plate, with a white cat on one side and a tiny black snail across from it on the other side of what the blue glaze suggests as a minuscule pond.

These postcards are aides mémoires of the porcelains in the show. And of others, too, of which there were no cards available. The monumental coupe, the size of a baptismal font, or the demitasse in the semi-circular shape of a vertically sliced half of a round cup.

I will keep these for a while, months or even years. They will become, during that time, mine. And one day, when I have the right kind of message to send the right kind of friend, it may be possible for me to part with one of them.

The recipient of such a card, a thank you note maybe, will not have occasion to take offense, for he will have received something of mine, a legitimate gift.

If, at this moment, I knew what that occasion or that person might be, the transaction would be calculated and, ever so slightly, corrupted.

꽃

Can a thought corrupt?

But of course! I bought my grandchildren Babar postcards, cute representations of elephants in their suits and dresses on their way to Paris. In one, they are in a balloon basket and in the other, they are in a primitive two-seater plane.

But I see now that I have mailed these cards that they are obviously Malinese!

Large, dark, looking silly in their excessively formal clothing (spats, even), they are the Africans who came from the jungle and began appearing in Paris in the late twenties and early thirties on their diplomatic missions. It would be impolite to say anything rude of them, but we may transmogrify them into figures for children that convey something of our sense of their absurdity here.

Jean de Brunhoff wrote his first Babar book in 1931.

꽃

A title of one of the volumes on a boukiniste's display along the river: I'm au Quai, You're au Quai.

This is the kind of self-help book that keeps people from going in Seine.

꽃

It is possible that I may never send my Limoges cards. Upon my death, in the great cleaning out of the accumulated books, papers, and the detritus of a life, someone—one of those grandchildren, perhaps—will find the shoe box in which I stashed away this very unsystematic collection.

The hand will hesitate for a moment, and then, as mine did once, light.

— Look at this saliére. Look at this dish with the cat and the snail.

— So?

— They're cute.

— Evidently grandpa thought so.

— Keep them?

— Sure.

That, let us agree, is the real Postcard Heaven.